ICONS

COLORS

SIGNS

TASCHEN

HONG KONG KÖLN LONDON LOS ANGELES MADRID PARIS TOKYO

Sumario
Sommario
Conteúdo

Introducción
Introduzione
Introdução

Los antiguos romanos utilizaban señales de tráfico para informar del trecho que mediaba entre diferentes partes de su imperio y Roma. Y, hasta el siglo XX, las señales experimentaron pocos cambios: indicaban la dirección y la distancia. Luego llegaron los coches, aumentó la velocidad y, de pronto, las señales se hicieron indispensables para la seguridad de todos. Lo conductores tenían que saber hacia dónde ir, los peligros que les acechaban, lo que otros usuarios de la carretera iban a hacer, y tenían que saberlo de forma rápida y sencilla. Así que comenzaron a aparecer círculos, triángulos, rectángulos y octógonos decorados con símbolos. Cuando los coches comenzaron a multiplicarse, las señales de tráfico del mundo se convirtieron en el único lenguaje verdaderamente internacional, creado para que cualquiera, en cualquier parte, pudiera entenderlo. Pero, aunque hasta las señales específicas de un país (no se ven muchas señales de «cruce de koalas» en Noruega) suelen ser fáciles de comprender, ello no significa que no vayas a necesitar ayuda en algunos casos. Nos gustaría que este libro fuera una guía del lenguaje de las señales de tráfico, en previsión de tu próximo viaje por carretera. Cuando hayas terminado de leerlo sabrás exactamente a qué peligros te expones, se trate de un canguro o de una mina terrestre.

Gli antichi romani usavano la segnaletica stradale per indicare le distanze fino a Roma dalle varie parti dell'impero. E fino al ventesimo secolo i segnali non sono cambiati un granché: limitandosi a mostrare la direzione e quanta strada bisognava fare. Poi, sono arrivate le macchine, la velocità è aumentata e, improvvisamente, la segnaletica è diventata essenziale per la sicurezza di tutti. Gli automobilisti dovevano sapere dove andare, quali pericoli li aspettavano sul cammino, cosa avrebbero fatto gli altri utenti della strada... e queste informazioni dovevano essere semplici e immediate. Così sono cominciati a spuntare tutti quei cerchi, triangoli, rettangoli e ottagoni decorati di simboli.

Quando le macchine hanno invaso il pianeta, la segnaletica è diventata l'unica vera lingua internazionale, creata per essere comprensibile ovunque e a chiunque. Malgrado i segnali prettamente locali (non ti capiterà di vedere molti pannelli di «attraversamento koala» in Norvegia) siano per lo più di facile comprensione, ciò non toglie che potresti aver bisogno d'aiuto. Ci piace pensare a questo libro come a una guida sul linguaggio della segnaletica stradale, per prepararti al tuo prossimo viaggio. Quando avrai finito di leggerlo, saprai esattamente in quali pericoli potresti incappare, se un canguro o una mina antiuomo.

Os antigos Romanos utilizavam os sinais de trânsito para indicar a distância até Roma das diferentes zonas do seu império. E até ao século XX, os sinais não mudaram muito: apenas indicavam o caminho e aquilo que se tinha de percorrer até lá chegar. Depois, chegaram os carros, as velocidades aumentaram e de repente os sinais tornaram-se essenciais para a segurança de todos. Os condutores precisavam de saber para onde se dirigir, que perigos os esperavam, aquilo que os outros utilizadores da estrada iam fazer, e tinham de saber isto de forma rápida e simples. Foi assim que começaram a surgir círculos, triângulos, rectângulos e octógonos decorados com símbolos. Quando os carros se espalharam por todo o mundo, os sinais de trânsito tornaram-se a única linguagem verdadeiramente internacional, criada de modo a que qualquer pessoa, em qualquer parte do mundo, a pudesse compreender. Apesar de, mesmo os sinais específicos de cada país (não é costume ver muitos sinais a dizer «zona de passagem de coalas» na Noruega), normalmente serem fáceis de perceber, isto não significa que por vezes não precisemos de ajuda. Gostaríamos de apresentar este livro como um guia para a linguagem dos sinais de trânsito, uma preparação para a próxima vez que te fizeres à estrada. Quando o acabares de o er, saberás interpretar com exactidão todos os perigos que possas ter de enfrentar, quer se trata de um canguru ou de uma mina terrestre.

7
Animales
Animali
Animais

Carreteras asesinas
Morti stradali
Morte na estrada

Supongamos que eres una tortuga establecida en el sur de Lituania. Y que llevas todo el año esperando el comienzo de la época del apareamiento. Supongamos que tu especie se traslada a la misma zona de reproducción desde hace 50.000 años, por lo que ya puede comenzar a considerarse una tradición. Este año inicias tu peregrinación y resulta que tropiezas con un obstáculo inesperado: una flamante autopista. Jamás has cruzado una y sientes cierta aprensión. ¿Qué haces?

Antes de lanzarte a cruzarla deberías conocer unas cuantas estadísticas. La mortalidad de ciervos en las carreteras estadounidenses es 6 veces superior a la causada por los cazadores. En el Reino Unido unos 100.000 conejos, 100.000 erizos, 47.000 tejones y 5.000 búhos son víctimas de las carreteras. Y se calcula que un 30 por ciento de la población anfibia (incluido 1 millón de sapos) queda cada año despanzurrada bajo las ruedas del tráfico.

Estas cifras te parecerán quizás desalentadoras, pero antes de dar media vuelta y volverte a casa deberías sopesar otro argumento. La época del apareamiento es muy importante para vosotras las tortugas. Cuando los ciclos reproductivos de una especie son perturbados, ésta corre el riesgo de extinguirse. De forma que, como se estima que cada año se extinguen unas 20.000 especies, tus colegas tortugas cuentan contigo.

Así que quizá será mejor que te decidas a cruzar la carretera y a asumir los riesgos. Al fin y al cabo, las carreteras forman parte integrante del paisaje; actualmente existen más de 22 millones de kilómetros de calzadas en el planeta (equivalentes a 28 veces el trayecto de ida y vuelta a la luna), y siguen construyéndose más cada día. Las autopistas de hoy en día podrían incluso influir en la evolución animal; según ciertas fuentes, las nuevas generaciones de erizos británicos están genéticamente adaptadas a huir de los coches en lugar de limitarse a enrollarse sobre sí mismos, como solían hacer (la tradicional reacción del erizo). En Venezuela, las iguanas verdes han integrado la carretera en sus ritos de apareamiento: cuando dos machos rivales pelean por una hembra, el perdedor tiene que cruzar la carretera y comenzar una nueva vida del otro lado.

Así que importa poco que las tortugas lleven viviendo 200 millones de años entre nosotros, porque las carreteras son una realidad insoslayable. Y si tu especie pretende sobrevivir no tendrá más remedio que aprender a mirar a ambos lados antes de cruzar.

Prova a metterti nei panni di una testuggine che vive nel sud della Lituania. Hai aspettato tutto l'anno, trepidante, la stagione degli amori. Sono 50.000 anni che la tua specie torna sempre nello stesso posto per accoppiarsi: è diventata una tradizione. Quest'anno, però, al momento di metterti in marcia t'imbatti in un ostacolo imprevisto: un'autostrada nuova di zecca. Non ne hai mai attraversata una e ti senti un po' in apprensione. Che fare?

Prima di decidere di attraversare la strada, ecco alcune statistiche da non trascurare: il numero di cervi uccisi ogni anno sulle autostrade statunitensi è sei volte superiore agli esemplari abbattuti dai cacciatori; lungo le strade britanniche vengono feriti ogni anno circa 100.000 conigli, 100.000 porcospini, 47.000 tassi e 5.000 barbagianni, mentre circa il 30 per cento degli anfibi (tra cui più di un milione di rospi) rimane spappolato sull'asfalto.

Questi dati potrebbero sembrarti alquanto deprimenti, ma prima di fare dietro front per tornarte-

SLOW
PENGUINS
CROSSING

NEXT 15 km

FOR
20
km

CROSSING
AHEAD

ne a casa pensaci bene. La stagione degli amori è molto importante per voi, care testuggini: lo sconvolgimento dei cicli riproduttivi, infatti, può determinare l'estinzione di una specie e, visto che ogni anno ne scompaiono circa 20.000, i tuoi simili contano su di te.

Forse, allora, la cosa migliore è attraversare la strada e rischiare il tutto per tutto. Del resto, al giorno d'oggi le autostrade sono una costante del paesaggio: sulla terra ci sono oltre 22 milioni di chilometri di strade (abbastanza per fare 28 viaggi di andata e ritorno sulla Luna) e il loro numero aumenta di giorno in giorno. Sembra addirittura che le moderne autostrade stiano influenzando l'evoluzione del regno animale. Secondo alcune fonti, in Gran Bretagna la nuova generazione di porcospini ha sviluppato una predisposizione genetica che li porta a fuggire di fronte alle auto in arrivo anziché appallottolarsi (la reazione istintiva). In Venezuela l'autostrada è entrata addirittura a far parte dei rituali di accoppiamento delle iguane verdi: quando i maschi rivali combattono durante la stagione degli amori, lo sconfitto deve attraversare la carreggiata e cominciare una nuova vita dall'altro lato della strada.

Quindi, non importa se le testuggini vivono su questo pianeta da 200 milioni di anni, le autostrade sono destinate a restare. Se la tua specie intende sopravvivere, vi conviene imparare a guardare da entrambi i lati prima di attraversare.

És uma tartaruga com casa, por exemplo, no sul da Lituânia. Tens estado ansiosamente à espera da época de acasalamento o ano inteiro. Há 50.000 anos que a tua espécie volta ao mesmo local de reprodução, portanto, é uma espécie de tradição. Mas, ao começares a tua caminhada este ano, deparas-te com um obstáculo inesperado: uma auto-estrada novinha em folha. Nunca atravessaste nenhuma e estás um bocado apreensiva. O que hás de fazer?

Antes de decidires atravessar a estrada, aqui vão algumas estatísticas importantes. As auto-estradas americanas matam seis vezes mais veados por ano do que os caçadores. No Reino Unido, cerca de 100.000 coelhos, 100.000 ouriços-cacheiros, 47.000 texugos e 5.000 mochos reais são vítimas das estradas todos os anos e, aproximadamente, 30 por cento da população anfíbia (incluindo mais de um milhão de sapos) é espalmada.

Estes números poderão parecer um pouco desanimadores, mas antes de dares meia volta e voltares para casa, há um outro aspecto a ter em conta. O período de acasalamento é muito importante para vocês, tartarugas. Quando os ciclos reprodutivos são quebrados, as espécies correm risco de extinção. E tendo em conta que cerca de 20.000 espécies desaparecem a cada ano, as tuas companheiras tartarugas precisam de ti para a sobrevivência da espécie.

Portanto, se calhar é melhor atravessares a estrada e correres o risco. No fim de contas, as auto-estradas constituem uma característica permanente da paisagem. Há mais de 22 milhões de quilómetros de estrada no planeta (suficientes para ir até à lua e voltar 28 vezes), e todos os dias se constróem mais. As auto-estradas de hoje podem inclusive estar a influenciar a evolução dos animais. De acordo com algumas fontes, uma nova geração de ouriços-cacheiros britânicos está geneticamente predisposta a fugir dos carros, em vez de se enrolar como uma bola (a reacção tradicional dos ouriços-cacheiros). Na Venezuela, as iguanas verdes passaram até a integrar as auto-estradas nos seus rituais de acasalamento: quando os machos rivais lutam por uma fêmea, aquele que perde deverá atravessar a estrada e começar uma nova vida do outro lado.

Portanto, o que é que interessa se as tartarugas existem há 200 milhões de anos? As auto-estradas vieram para ficar. Se a tua espécie pretender sobreviver, mais vale aprender a olhar para os dois lados antes de atravessar.

ETC.
NEXT
25km

1 km

TURTLES CAN BITE
PLEASE DO NOT TOUCH THEM

CAUTION
WATER DRAGON HABITAT

BEWARE
ATTACKING
BIRDS

REDUCE SPEED
AHEAD
WILDLIFE CROSSING
THANK YOU

BEZIHAMBEL
"QAWUL'...INQWENYA"

暴龍地帶
請照顧同行之小童
Tyrannosaurus Rex Roaring Ahead
May frighten young children

Don't feed the seagulls
They become aggressive
and will steal food.

PRECAUCION
REDUZ
VELOCIDAD

HIGH IMP
WATCH FO
SPEED IS
Road Sense
ICBC
Province of British Colu
Ministry of Transportati

CT AREA
WILDLIFE
LING US
ways
Cranbrook & District
Traffic Safety Commitee

23

Hombre
Uomo
Homen

¿Por dónde vamos?
Avanti dove?
Para onde vamos

Todo comenzó con la amenaza de la violencia, o eso parece. El lado de la carretera en el que conducimos depende del lado del cuerpo en el que nuestros ancestros llevaban la espada. Cuando los hombres comenzaron a desplazarse, en una época en que los caminos estaban plagados de mercachifles y de salteadores, la prudencia dictaba caminar por el lado de la senda donde más fácil resultaba defenderse. De forma que un hombre diestro (es probable que pocas mujeres viajaran solas y armadas con espada) prefería permanecer en el lado izquierdo, donde podía desenvainar antes la espada —que llevaba en el lado izquierdo del cuerpo— con la mano derecha. Aunque si uno conducía un carro, era costumbre ir sentado en la parte de dentro de la carretera y por lo tanto conducir por la derecha (manejar un carro y llevar una espada debía ser un lío). Napoleón decretó que la gente condujera por la derecha, aunque no todos los países que había conquistado le obedecieron. Lo que podría explicar el estado actual del asunto; 163 países conducen por la derecha y 58 por la izquierda. Aunque esta situación puede ser cambiante. Como en Suecia, que decidió en 1967 cambiar de lado para adecuarse a las normas del resto de Europa continental a pesar de que 12 años antes el 82,9 por ciento de la población hubiera declarado sentirse feliz conduciendo por la izquierda. El cambio necesitó una semana y mucha prudencia, pero no hubo víctimas mortales. En otros lugares siguen existiendo puntos negros donde no se sabe a qué lado mirar entre países fronterizos: intenta conducir entre Paquistán y China, Tailandia y Laos, Namibia y Angola, o llegar a Europa procedente de las Islas Británicas. Aunque, al igual que cuando sólo había carros y espadas, el peligro principal no estriba en qué lado de la carretera se conduce, sino en los conductores: cada año mueren más de 1,2 millones de personas en las carreteras del mundo.

Tutto cominciò sotto la minaccia della violenza, o almeno così raccontano. Il lato di guida dipende dal lato del corpo in cui i nostri antenati portavano la spada. Quando si diffuse l'abitudine di viaggiare, le strade pullulavano di venditori ambulanti e briganti, e camminando sul bordo della strada era più facile difendersi. Perciò, un uomo destrorso (non dovevano esserci molte donne armate di spada che se ne andavano da sole in giro per il mondo) preferiva tenersi sulla sinistra, cioè il lato migliore per raggiungere il fodero (che si trovava in genere a sinistra) con la mano destra. Il conducente di un calesse, invece, di solito stava seduto sul lato interno della strada, guidando quindi a destra (chi stava alla guida di un carro con una spada al fianco non doveva avere le idee molto chiare). Napoleone impose la guida a destra, ma non tutti i paesi conquistati obbedirono. Il che può spiegare l'attuale stato delle cose: 163 paesi a destra e 58 a sinistra. Ma non sono da escludere repentine inversioni di marcia. La Svezia, ad esempio, decise di cambiare lato nel 1967 per adeguarsi al resto del continente europeo, anche se 12 anni prima l'82,9 per cento della popolazione si dichiarava soddisfatto della guida a sinistra. Per portare a termine questa vera e propria rivoluzione ci volle appena una settimana e molte assidue lezioni di guida, ma non ci furono vittime. Nel resto del mondo esistono ancora una serie di fantomatici «punti della morte», in prossimità delle frontiere fra paesi che hanno diversi lati di guida: prova a farti un giro in macchina fra il Pakistan e la Cina, la Thailandia e il Laos, la Namibia e

BAH
Ampel K
SURA
AMPEL
TELP. 5617

l'Angola, o ad arrivare in Europa dalle Isole Britanniche. Eppure, proprio come all'epoca in cui c'erano solo spade e carri, il vero pericolo non è tanto il lato di guida, ma chi incontri sul cammino: più di 1,2 milioni di persone vengono uccise ogni anno sulle strade di tutto il mondo.

Tudo começou com a ameaça da violência ou, pelo menos, é o que se pensa. O lado da estrada pelo qual conduzimos depende do lado do corpo em que os nossos antepassados transportavam a espada. Quando as pessoas se começaram a movimentar, numa altura em que as estradas estavam invadidas por vendedores ambulantes e salteadores, compensava andar pelo lado em que uma pessoa se pudesse defender melhor. Assim, um homem destro (provavelmente não havia muitas mulheres a andar com espadas e a viajar sozinhas) preferia ficar do lado esquerdo, para poder chegar melhor à bainha da espada – que transportava no lado esquerdo do corpo – com a sua mão direita. Se uma pessoa, porém, estivesse a conduzir uma carroça, era costume ela sentar-se no sentido do interior da estrada e, assim, andar pela direita (se estivesses a conduzir uma carroça e a transportar uma espada, provavelmente ficarias um bocado confuso). Napoleão decretou que as pessoas andassem pela direita, mas nem todos os países que conquistou o obedeceram, o que poderá explicar o estado actual da situação – 163 países conduzem pela direita e 58 pela esquerda. No entanto, estes valores não são necessariamente permanentes. Repara só no caso da Suécia, que em 1967 decidiu mudar de lado para ficar igual ao resto da Europa continental, apesar de 12 anos antes 82,9 por cento da população ter dito que estava contente por guiar à esquerda. A mudança demorou uma semana e uma preparação muito cuidadosa, mas não houve fatalidades. Noutros lugares ainda existem zonas de incerteza, ou «buracos negros», entre países fronteiriços: experimenta conduzir entre o Paquistão e a China, entre a Tailândia e o Laos, entre a Namíbia e Angola, ou chegar à Europa vindo das Ilhas Britânicas. Mas, tal como no tempo em que apenas havia carroças e espadas, não é bem o lado da estrada em que se guia que constitui o principal perigo, e sim as pessoas que conduzem: todos os anos, mais de 1,2 milhões de pessoas morrem nas estradas do nosso planeta.

XING

9h30 – 10h30
LUNDI
JEUDI
1 MARS AU 1 DEC
ARRÊT

35

Alto

Stop

Pare

Octógono
Ottagono
Octógono

La señal de STOP, que se estrenó en Estados Unidos en 1915, es actualmente la única señal de tráfico oficial que las normas internacionales permiten tener una forma octogonal.

La señal es así no sólo por razones de seguridad: esta forma requiere más recortes (y por lo tanto más desperdicios) que los acostumbrados cuadrados, triángulos o círculos. Mientras que la forma pudo decidirse un poco a la ligera, conseguir el diseño final costó un poco más. Al principio las letras eran negras sobre un fondo blanco, pero cambiaron rápidamente a negras sobre amarillo y luego a rojas sobre amarillo antes de convertirse en la famosa rotulación blanca sobre fondo rojo. En Estados Unidos, la señal tiene ahora reflectores *ojo de gato*, una medida estándar de 76,2 cm por 76,2 cm y debería estar montada a una altura de 2,1 metros. Y ahora está en todas partes. Aunque en los países de habla hispana de Sudamérica y América central la señal sigue ostentando un PARE o ALTO en español, España utiliza la señal anglosajona de STOP. Aunque no es culpa del país sino de los reglamentos de la Unión Europea.

Dopo il debutto negli Usa, nel 1915, oggi il segnale dello STOP è l'unico pannello ufficiale a forma ottogonale di tutta la segnaletica stradale internazionale.

Il segnale è unico nel suo genere non solo per motivi di sicurezza: questa forma geometrica deve essere tagliata in modo più elaborato (e ciò aumenta gli sprechi) rispetto ai più inflazionati quadrati, triangoli e cerchi. E se la scelta della forma è stata rapida, per la grafica le cose sono andate per le lunghe. All'inizio la scritta era nera su sfondo bianco, ma cambiò ben presto in nero su giallo, per poi diventare rossa in campo giallo, prima di approdare infine al celebre bianco su sfondo rosso. Oggi negli Stati Uniti il pannello ha tanto di catarifrangenti, con dimensioni standard di 76,2 x 76,2 cm e deve essere montato a un'altezza di 2,1 m. E ormai ha conquistato tutto il pianeta. Solo nei paesi di lingua ispanica dell'America Latina continua a riportare la dicitura spagnola «PARE» o «ALTO», mentre la Spagna ha adottato l'inglese STOP. Suo malgrado, però: questo anglicismo è stato introdotto soltanto per ottemperare a una normativa dell'Unione europea.

Tendo estreado pela primeira vez nos EUA em 1915, o sinal de STOP é hoje o único sinal de trânsito oficial internacionalmente estabelecido que possui uma forma octogonal.

Este sinal é único por razões que ultrapassam as meramente relacionadas com a segurança: a sua forma implica a realização de mais cortes (e portanto de mais desperdício) do que os sinais de forma quadrada, triangular e circular mais comuns. Se, por um lado, a sua forma terá sido decidida rapidamente, a escolha do *design* final demorou mais tempo. Ao princípio, consistia em letras pretas sobre um fundo branco, tendo rapidamente mudado para letras pretas sobre um fundo amarelo, e depois para letras vermelhas sobre um fundo amarelo, antes de acabar por ficar com letras brancas sobre um fundo vermelho. Actualmente, nos EUA, estes sinais possuem reflectores catadióptricos, com um tamanho standard de 76,2 cm por 76,2 cm e devem ser colocados à altura de 2,1 m. É um sinal que hoje se vê no mundo inteiro. Enquanto os sinais existentes nos países de língua espanhola da América Central e do Sul ainda têm a palavra espanhola «PARE» ou «ALTO,» a própria Espanha utiliza o STOP inglês. No entanto, a culpa não é do país, pois Espanha apenas se limitou a satisfazer os requisitos dos regulamentos da União Europeia.

TOW AWAY
NO
PARKING
THIS
SIDE
STOP

STOP

PARE
STOP
STOP
หยุด
قف
STOP
정지
STOP
STOP
停
DUR
STOP
4 WAY

STOP
ቁም
قف
STOP
หยุด
STOP
STOP
ຢຸດ
ឈប់
STOP
STOP
STOP

43

Perro
Cane
Cão

Manjar canino
Carne canina
Comida canina

Un hombre saca a un dálmata de la perrera y lo arrastra por un callejón trasero del mercado Chilsung de Taegu (Corea del Sur). El perro defeca de pánico cuando la cuerda que le ciñe el pescuezo se estrecha. Seguidamente, el hombre introduce en la boca del perro una varilla metálica conectada a un generador y lo somete a una descarga eléctrica que encrespa el cuerpo del animal. El proceso se repite varias veces. Aturdido pero todavía con vida, el perro deberá soportar que el hombre lo soase luego con un soplete y lo deje sin pelaje. La totalidad de la operación dura una hora. El objetivo es que el perro segregue la mayor cantidad posible de adrenalina en el momento de la muerte. Se cree que la carne rica en adrenalina es un poderoso afrodisíaco que permite largas erecciones a los hombres. La mayoría de los 2 millones de perros que se consumen anualmente en Corea del Sur se asan a la parrilla o entran en la receta de la *youngyangtang* (sopa de la salud), y se venden al precio de 20.000 won/kilo (16 $US). Así como la carne se estropea rápidamente si no se refrigera, la erección, según la leyenda, puede durar horas.

Un dalmata viene trascinato fuori dalla sua gabbia e portato in un vicolo dietro al mercato Chilsung aTaegu, in Corea del Sud. Mentre la corda si stringe sempre di più attorno al collo, il cane defeca per lo shock. Poi gli viene infilata in bocca una sbarra metallica collegata a un generatore di scariche elettriche e per un'ora intera il corpo dell'animale, stordito ma non ancora morto, viene ustionato con una fiamma ossidrica che gli brucia il pelo. Tutto ciò allo scopo di far produrre al cane la maggiore quantità possibile di adrenalina al momento della morte. La carne ad alto contenuto di adrenalina è considerata un potente afrodisiaco in grado di prolungare l'erezione negli uomini. La maggior parte dei due milioni di cani che vengono mangiati in Corea del Sud ogni anno vengono fatti arrosto o trasformati in *youngyangtang* (zuppa della salute) e venduti al prezzo di 20.000 won (US$16) al chilo. Mentre la carne non si conserva a lungo fuori dal frigorifero, l'erezione, stando alla leggenda, può durare per ore.

Um Dálmata é arrastado de uma jaula para um beco sem saída, por trás do mercado Chilsung, em Taegu, na Coreia do Sul. Com uma corda a apertar-lhe o pescoço, o cão defeca devido ao choque. Uma vara de metal ligada a um gerador eléctrico é enfiada na sua boca e a electricidade invade-lhe o esqueleto. Este processo é repetido várias vezes. Atordoado, mas ainda vivo, toda a sua pele é queimada com um maçarico, enquanto é retirada. Tudo isto demora uma hora. O objectivo é fazer o cão segregar o máximo de adrenalina possível no momento da morte. Acredita-se que a carne rica em adrenalina constitui um poderoso afrodisíaco capaz de proporcionar ao homem erecções muito longas. A maioria dos dois milhões de cães que são comidos anualmente na Coreia do Sul são assados ou utilizados para a preparação da *youngyangtang* (sopa saudável) e vendidos por 20.000 wons (US$16) o quilo. Se por um lado a carne se estraga depressa se não for conservada a frio, a erecção, diz a voz do povo, pode durar horas e horas.

BEWARE
OF
DOG
OUT
BOOFHEAD
BEWARE
THIS AREA IS PROTECTED BY
GUARD DOGS

BEWARE OF THE DOG
BHASOBHA INJA

ATTENTI
AL CANE
E AL PADRONE

honden
aanlijnen
beslist geen
hondenpoep
VERBODEN TOEGANG
ART. 461 WETB. V. STRAFR.

J'AIME
MON QUARTIER
JE RAMASSE
RÈGLEMENT SANITAIRE DÉPARTEMENTAL ART. 99-2
INFRACTION PUNIE PAR UNE AMENDE
POUVANT ATTEINDRE 3000F (457€)

IO NON POSSO ENTRARE

POUSS

IO, DEVO
ESSERE TENUTO
AL GUINZAGLIO
E PORTARE LA
MUSERUOLA

SPORTS AREA
DOGS PROHIBITED
PER EVIDENTI RAGIONI DI IGIENE E' VIETATO INTRODURRE ANIMALI NEI LOCALI DI VENDITA
HUNDEVERBOT

Med særlig
tilladelse

55

Transporte
Trasporto
Transporte

Vehículo bendecido
Sant'automobile
A bênção de carros

En el templo Zenkoji de Nagano (Japón), los sacerdotes budistas se encargan de bendecir los coches (en la tarifa de 5.000 ¥, 46 $US, va incluido un amuleto de madera que se cuelga del retrovisor). Los sacerdotes católicos bendicen a veces oficialmente los automóviles (aunque en Francia un obispo ha pedido que se ponga fin a este ritual supersticioso). Los taxistas kenianos prefieren en cambio pintar una plegaria sobre sus vehículos. «Pedimos a Dios que nos proteja de los peligros de nuestras carreteras», dice Robert Maina Kamanda, de Bombolulu (su taxi exhibe la frase *El Señor es mi pastor*, en suajili). «Me siento más seguro, porque la Biblia dice *Pide y se te concederá*».

Nel tempio di Zenkoji a Nagano, in Giappone, i sacerdoti buddisti sono specializzati in benedizioni automobilistiche (la tariffa di ¥5.000, pari a US$46, è comprensiva di un talismano di legno da appendere allo specchietto retrovisore). Anche i sacerdoti cattolici a volte benedicono ufficialmente le macchine (benché un vescovo francese abbia invitato a farla finita con questi riti di «magia spicciola»). I tassisti in Kenya si limitano a scrivere una preghiera sulla carrozzeria. «Chiediamo a Dio di proteggerci dai pericoli delle nostre strade», spiega Robert Maina Kamanda, di Bombolulu (il suo taxi è decorato con la scritta «Il Signore è il mio pastore» in swahili). «Così mi sento più sicuro perché la Bibbia dice 'Chiedi e ti sarà dato'.»

No Templo Zenkoji, em Nagano, no Japão, os monges budistas estão a especializar-se na bênção de carros (a tarifa de ¥5.000, US$46, inclui um talismã de madeira para pendurar no espelho retrovisor). Por vezes, os padres católicos benzem formalmente os carros (mas em França um bispo apelou ao fim deste ritual «hocus-pocus»). Os taxistas do Quénia limitam-se a pintar uma prece no seu veículo. «Pedimos a Deus que nos proteja dos perigos das nossas estradas», diz Robert Maina Kamanda, de Bombolulu (o seu táxi está decorado com a seguinte frase em swahili «O Senhor é o meu pastor»). «Sinto-me mais seguro porque a Bíblia diz, 'Pede e ser-te-á dado.'»

WHEN
WET

CUANDO
LLUEVE

A 300 m

SLIPPERY
WHEN WET

AJF-7292

NEW SEAL

Ganarse la vida
Trasgressione
Quebrando as regras

Sólo 12 de cada 1.000 nigerianos poseen un coche. Lo que conlleva que el transporte público sea un negocio altamente lucrativo. «El sistema de transporte está controlado aquí por bandas mafiosas», dice Seye Solola, un conductor de autobús de Lagos. Las bandas más terribles son las llamadas *agbero* [gancho] que se dedican a extorsionar a los conductores. Los *ganchos* se quejan de no merecer su mala reputación; no hacen más que su trabajo. «En tanto que *oficial de aparcamiento de vehículos motorizados* actúo de recaudador de tasas», dice Sulaimon Atere, de 26 años. «No puedo decir si las tasas que cobramos son legales o no. Los *ganchos* somos antiguos conductores en el paro; como no tenemos trabajo debemos encontrar una forma de ganarnos la vida. Y no nos queda más remedio que ser violentos porque los conductores se nos resisten cuando nos acercamos a ellos en son de paz».

Solo 12 nigeriani su 1.000 possiedono una macchina: ecco perché i trasporti pubblici sono un affare molto redditizio. «Il sistema dei trasporti, qui da noi, è controllato dalle gang», racconta Seye Solola, autista di autobus a Lagos. Le gang più temibili sono chiamate *agbero* [gli abusivi] ed estorcono soldi ai conducenti con la forza. Ma gli abusivi si lamentano: a detta loro non meritano questa cattiva reputazione, stanno soltanto facendo il loro lavoro. «In veste di 'addetto ai parcheggi stradali' agisco come un esattore delle tasse», spiega Sulaimon Atere, 26 anni. «Non so dirti se la tassa che riscuotiamo sia legale o illegale. Gli abusivi sono persone che prima facevano i conducenti, e dato che ora siamo senza lavoro dobbiamo inventarci un modo per guadagnarci da vivere. Siamo costretti a essere violenti perché gli automobilisti fanno resistenza se li prendiamo con le buone.»

Apenas 12 de cada 1.000 nigerianos possui um carro. Isto torna os transportes públicos num negócio lucrativo. «Aqui, o sistema de transportes é controlado por gangs,» diz Seye Solola, um condutor de autocarros de Lagos. Os gangs mais terríveis chamam-se *agbero* [angariadores] e extorquem dinheiro aos condutores à força. Os angariadores queixam-se dizendo que não merecem essa má reputação. Estão apenas a fazer o seu trabalho. «Como 'funcionário do parque automóvel' actuo como um cobrador de impostos,» diz Sulaimon Atere, de 26 anos. «Não posso dizer que o imposto que cobramos seja legal ou ilegal. Os angariadores são antigos condutores; como estamos sem trabalho, temos de arranjar uma maneira de ganhar a vida. Temos de ser violentos pois os condutores oferecem resistência quando os abordamos de forma pacífica».

30м

TAKSI
K/T LIETUVA
ACOMODADOR
TAXI
タクシー
のりば
東光電気工事
op !

Perigo !

НА ВЛАДИМИР
1
BUSES
PARADA
ช่องเดินรถ
ประจำทาง
ตลอดเวลา

ویگن سٹاپ
مِلٹری پولیس

PARADA

Camioneros cansados
Camionisti stanchi
Os camionistas cansados

Una tercera parte de los accidentes mortales de camión se deben al cansancio (suelen producirse entre las 3 y las 5 de la madrugada). Así que no es de extrañar que permanecer despierto sea una obsesión para la mayoría de los camioneros de largos recorridos. En Kenia, muchos de ellos mascan hojas de *qat*, un estimulante adictivo ilegal. Los camioneros tailandeses prefieren fumar *ya maa*, una poderosa anfetamina, aunque poseer una pastilla puede conllevar una pena de 5 años de cárcel y una multa de 50.000 baht (1.250 $US). Pero la seguridad pública pasa detrás de las exigencias económicas. «Cuando trabajo tengo que tomarlas porque, de lo contrario, me duermo», dice Thon, de 37 años, que conduce camiones en el norte de Tailandia durante la zafra de la caña de azúcar, entre diciembre y marzo, y que consigue dormir 4 o 5 horas diarias. Aunque la reglamentación estadounidense exige que los camioneros duerman 8 horas diarias, las autoridades tailandesas prefieren ignorar el tema. Porque, como dice Thon, «La policía no intervendría dado que el azúcar se exporta a países extranjeros».

Un terzo degli incidenti mortali sui camion è dovuto alla stanchezza (di solito fra le 3 e le 5 del mattino). Non stupisce quindi che la maggior parte dei camionisti che macinano lunghe distanze abbia la fissazione di restare sveglia. In Kenya molti masticano foglie di *khat*, un eccitante illegale che crea assuefazione. I thailandesi, invece, preferiscono fumare la *ya maa*, una potente anfetamina, anche se basta essere trovati in possesso di una pasticca per beccarsi cinque anni di prigione e 50.000 baht (US$1.250) di multa. L'ordine pubblico passa in secondo piano rispetto alle leggi dell'economia. «Quando lavoro devo prenderla, altrimenti mi addormento», racconta Thon, 37 anni, che guida camion nel nord della Thailandia durante il raccolto della canna da zucchero (da dicembre a marzo) tirando avanti con 4-5 ore di sonno al giorno. E se la normativa statunitense impone otto ore di sonno giornaliere ai camionisti, le autorità thailandesi fanno finta di niente. Come spiega Thon: «La polizia non s'immischia perché lo zucchero viene esportato all'estero».

Um terço dos acidentes fatais com camiões são causados pela fadiga (normalmente entre as 3 e as 5 da manhã). Portanto, não é de admirar que para a maioria dos camionistas de percursos de longa distância manter-se acordado seja uma obsessão. No Quénia muitos mascam folha de khat, um estimulante ilegal e susceptível de causar dependência. Os camionistas tailandeses preferem fumar *ya maa*, uma poderosa anfetamina, apesar de a posse de uma barra poder representar uma sentença de cinco anos de prisão e uma multa de 50.000 bahts (US$1.250) para os ofensores. A segurança pública, no entanto, é uma prioridade secundária para a economia. «Quando trabalho, tenho de a consumir, senão adormeço», diz Thon, de 37 anos, que conduz camiões no norte da Tailândia durante a colheita de cana de açúcar, de Dezembro a Março. Ele vai-se desenrascando com quatro a cinco horas de sono por dia. Apesar dos regulamentos dos EU exigirem que os camionistas durmam oito horas por dia, as autoridades tailandesas preferem ignorar este facto. Tal como diz Thon, «A polícia não interfere porque o açúcar é exportado para o estrangeiro».

40
80
40
50

不可阻塞
KEEP CLEAR

4 t

w.newyorkpizza.
Herengracht 516 Tel.020-5252496

Parchimetro

自転車放置
禁止区域
渋谷区

फेरी वालों को अंदर जाना मना है
SLOW
CHILDREN

89

Niños
Bambini
Crianças

MA
SV

SOBRES - SOBRES

AA
SCHOOL

COLEGIO

Set An
Example !
Wait For Cross
Signal Opposite
ASB

線路に物を落とされた方は
駅係員にお申し出ください

Almuerzo escolar
Mensa scolastica
Almoço na escola

Las notas que dejan los alumnos en el buzón de sugerencias del comedor de la escuela Oakwood Friends School del Estado de Nueva York (EE UU) piden más alas de pollo asadas, más queso fundido y más patatas fritas. En Argentina, durante la crisis de 2001-2002, los escolares tuvieron menos opciones de menú. La debacle económica se saldó con el derrumbamiento de la divisa nacional y una inflación incontrolada que hizo que muchas familias pasaran hambre. «Muchas provincias han decidido mantener los comedores abiertos durante los fines de semana y los periodos de vacaciones», dijo entonces Mariano Mohadeb, del Ministerio de Educación argentino, «porque muchos chicos van a la escuela no sólo a estudiar sino a comer. Es el único lugar donde pueden conseguir comida». El ministerio destinó 5 millones de pesos (1,7 millones $US) para subvencionar el presupuesto de alimentación escolar en 10 provincias, esperando con ello poder ayudar a unos 800.000 niños en 6.000 escuelas. «Las escuelas siempre han desempeñado un enorme papel en la sociedad», declaró Mariano. «Un papel que todavía cobra mayor importancia en estos tiempos de crisis».

I bigliettini lasciati nella cassetta dei suggerimenti per la mensa scolastica alla Friends School di Oakwood, nello Stato di New York (Usa), chiedevano più ali di pollo e formaggio alla griglia e più patatine fritte. Durante il tracollo economico del 2001-2002 gli alunni delle scuole argentine si sono dovuti accontentare di un menù molto più limitato. A causa della crisi (la valuta è crollata, mentre il tasso d'inflazione saliva alle stelle) un numero ancora imprecisato di famiglie ha patito la fame. «Molte province hanno deciso di tenere aperte le mense scolastiche anche nel fine settimana e durante il periodo estivo», riferisce Mariano Mohadeb del ministero dell'Educazione argentino, «perché tantissimi bambini andavano a scuola non solo per studiare ma anche per sfamarsi. E quello era l'unico posto in cui potevano trovare qualcosa da mangiare.» Il ministero ha stanziato 5 milioni di pesos (1,7 milioni di dollari) per finanziare il programma alimentare scolastico in 10 province del paese, destinato ad aiutare circa 800.000 bambini in 6.000 istituti. «Le scuole hanno sempre svolto un grandissimo ruolo sociale», dice Mariano. «E oggi, in questi tempi di crisi, questo ruolo è diventato più essenziale che mai.»

Umas tiras de papel deixadas na caixa de sugestões para almoço da Oakwood Friends School, em Poughkeepsie, nos EUA, pediam mais asas de galinha no churrasco, queijo grelhado e batatas fritas. Durante a crise económica de 2001-2002, na Argentina, a variedade de comida nas escolas diminuiu. A crise, que provocou a desvalorização da moeda e a subida da inflação, levou a que um número desconhecido de famílias passassem fome. «Muitas províncias decidiram manter os refeitórios das escolas abertos durante os fins-de-semana e ao longo do verão», disse na altura Mariano Mohadeb, do Ministério de Educação Argentino, «porque muitas crianças vão à escola não só para estudar, mas também para comer. É o único lugar onde elas podem comer». O Ministério dispensou 5 milhões de pesos (US$1,7 milhões) para pagar um programa de alimentação escolar em 10 províncias, acreditando que isto ajudaria cerca de 800.000 crianças de 6.000 escolas. «As escolas desempenharam sempre um papel importantíssimo na sociedade», disse Mariano. «Hoje, em tempos de crise, o seu papel é mais importante do que nunca.»

បន្ថយ_ល្បឿន
20 K.M/h

CAUTION
SCHOOL CROSSING

RALENTIR

SCHOOL
CHILDREN CROSSING

40

School

ATTENTION ETUDIANTS

School
學校

Skole

30

ŠOLA
PLIN
ZP 160
22 T
30
PLIN
ZP 225
22 T
42
PLIN
ZP 160
T 09
35

Децата нямат
спирачки!
БИГ БЕН

سوبر

G.M.P
9 TO 12 HRS. 17 TO 20-30

111

Miscelánea
Miscellanea
Vários

WHEN YOU GO HOME
TELL THEM OF US
FOR THEIR TOMORROW
WE GAVE OUR TODAY

BORDER ROADS ORGANISATION
SLEEP YOUR FAMILY WILL WEEP

HIMANK PROJECT
SECTOR STARTS
WEL COME
LEH
251
UPSHI
202

BORDER ROADS ORGANISATION
SAVE ENVIRONMENT

WELCOME
TO
MOON LAND

MOREPLAIN
ENJOY NATURE
WHILE DRIVING

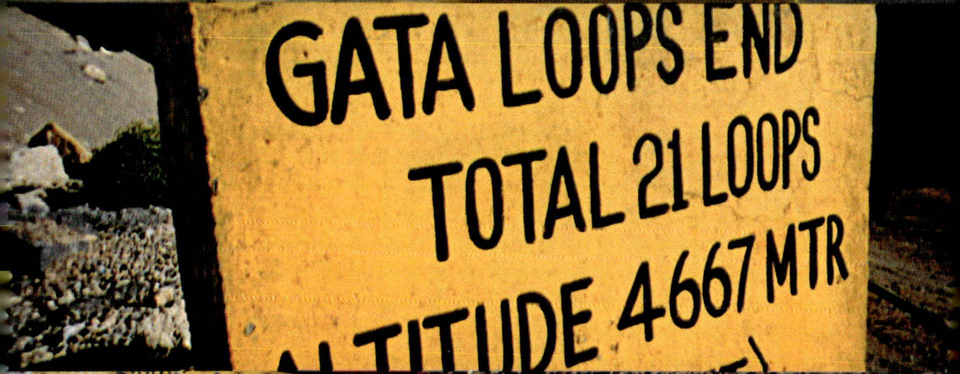
GATA LOOPS END
TOTAL 21 LOOPS
LTITUDE 4667 MTR

BORDER ROADS ORGANISATION
AST WON'T LAST
GREF
81

SOFT
SHOULDER

CREDITOS Y APARTADOS
OLYMPIA
BAZAR CHO

งานวางท่อประปาขนาด ø ซม.
เริ่มงาน แล้วเสร็จ
ดำเนินการโดย หจก. สามประสิทธิ์ โทร.243-0066
ควบคุมงานโดยนาย
โทร. 243-4726
การประปานครหลวงยินดีรับใช้ประชาชน
ห.จ.ก. สามประสิทธิ์

ห.จ.ก. สามประสิทธิ์

उ·ट्रा·प्र·का·
24 HOURS

123

Peligro

Pericolo

Perigo

Última cena
Ultimo pasto
Última ceia

A las 4h30 de la tarde del 30 de mayo de 2002 Stanley Allison Baker Jr. comenzó a comer dos solomillos de 500 gramos, 450 gramos de pavo en finas rodajas, 12 lonchas de beicon, dos hamburguesas con mayonesa, cebolla y lechuga, dos patatas grandes asadas con mantequilla, crema agria, queso y cebollino, cuatro lonchas de queso, una ensalada mixta aliñada con queso azul, dos mazorcas de maíz y un cubilete de helado de menta con pepitas de chocolate. Y bebió cuatro Coca-Colas de vainilla. A las 5h55 de la tarde Stanley fue conducido desde su celda del corredor de la muerte de la unidad Polunsky de Livingston, Texas (EE UU), a la cámara de la muerte de la cárcel de Huntsville, donde fue ejecutado mediante inyección letal —un cóctel químico de tiopental sódico (para sedar), de bromuro de pancuronio (para paralizar el diafragma y los pulmones) y de cloruro potásico (para detener el corazón)—.

La cárcel de Huntsville alberga la cámara de la muerte más ajetreada de Estados Unidos. En noviembre de 2002 habían sido ejecutadas en ella 31 personas (más de la mitad de las ejecuciones realizadas este año en el país). Procesar a Stanley ha costado al Estado de Texas unos 2,16 millones $US, una suma muchísimo más alta que el coste de un juicio sin pena de muerte (o equivalente a unas tres veces lo que cuesta encarcelar a una persona en una celda individual en una cárcel de máxima seguridad durante 40 años). Los juicios con pena de muerte son más largos y, como casi todos son automáticamente recurridos, los reos permanecen en el corredor de la muerte durante un promedio de 10 años y siete meses. Anular el derecho a recurrir supondría un ahorro presupuestario considerable pero podría acabar resultando muy caro: un estudio de la Facultad de derecho de la Universidad de Columbia del año 2000 puso de manifiesto que el 68 por ciento de los juicios con sentencia a la pena capital recurridos entre 1973 y 1995 tenían defectos tan graves que se habían tenido que celebrar de nuevo.

Alle 16.30 del 30 maggio 2002 Stanley Allison Baker Jr. comincia a mangiare: due bistecche con l'osso da 500 g; 450 g di tacchino affettato fine; 12 fette di pancetta affumicata; due hamburger con maionese, cipolla e lattuga; due grandi patate al cartoccio con burro, panna acida, formaggio ed erba cipollina; quattro fette di formaggio; un'insalata dello chef con salsa allo stilton; due pannocchie di granturco e un barattolo di gelato alla menta con pepite di cioccolato. Il tutto scolandosi quattro lattine di Coca-Cola al gusto di vaniglia. Alle 17.55 Stanley viene condotto dalla sua cella, nel braccio della morte dell'unità Polunsky a Livingston, in Texas (Usa), alla camera della morte della prigione di Huntsville, dove viene giustiziato con un'iniezione letale di un cocktail chimico a base di tiopentale sodico (per addormentare), bromuro di pancuronio (per interrompere l'attività del diaframma e dei polmoni) e cloruro di potassio (per arrestare il cuore).

La prigione di Huntsville ospita la camera della morte più trafficata degli Usa: nel novembre del 2002 contava al suo attivo 31 esecuzioni, cioè più della metà delle condanne a morte eseguite quell'anno nell'intero paese. Il procedimento legale contro Stanley è costato allo stato del Texas circa 2,16 milioni di dollari in più rispetto a un processo che non contemplasse la pena capitale (o circa il triplo della somma necessaria per tenere un detenuto in una cella singola di massima sicurezza per 40 anni). I processi in cui si decide una condanna a

KEBA LIWA

morte durano più a lungo e, dato che comportano quasi automaticamente un ricorso in appello, i detenuti rimangono in media nel braccio della morte per un periodo di 10 anni e 7 mesi. Sopprimendo il diritto di ricorso in appello si risparmierebbe denaro, ma il prezzo potrebbe essere molto alto: uno studio condotto nel 2000 dalla Columbia University Law School ha dimostrato che in sede di appello, fra il 1973 e il 1995, il 68 per cento delle sentenze di condanna a morte presentavano vizi talmente gravi da richiedere un nuovo processo o il riesame della pena.

Às 4:30 da tarde do dia 30 de Maio de 2002, Stanley Allison Baker Jr. começou a comer duas costeletas de novilho de 500 g, 450 g de peru cortado em fatias finas, 12 fatias de bacon, dois hamburgueres com maionese, cebola e alface, duas grandes batatas assadas com manteiga, natas, queijo e cebolinhas, quatro fatias de queijo, uma salada com molho cremoso, duas maçarocas de milho, e um balde de gelado de menta com pedaços de chocolate. Bebeu quatro coca-colas de baunilha. Às 5:55 da tarde, Stanley foi levado da sua cela no corredor da morte da unidade de Polunsky, em Livingston, no Texas, EUA, para a câmara da morte da prisão de Huntsville, onde foi executado por injecção letal – um cocktail químico de tiopental sódico (para sedar), brometo de pancurónio (para o colapso do diafragma e dos pulmões) e cloreto de potássio (para o coração).

A prisão de Huntsville é a câmara de morte com mais movimento dos EUA. Até Novembro de 2002, tinham sido lá executadas 31 pessoas – mais de metade das execuções do país. O processo contra Stanley custou ao estado do Texas cerca de US$2,16 milhões a mais do que o custo de um julgamento que não envolva a pena de morte (ou cerca de três vezes o custo de aprisionar alguém numa cela individual de alta segurança durante 40 anos). Os julgamentos de pena de morte duram mais tempo e, como se recorre quase automaticamente da sentença, os prisioneiros são mantidos no corredor da morte por uma média de 10 anos e 7 meses. Cortar o direito de recurso seria uma medida que pouparia dinheiro, mas o custo poderia ser elevado: um estudo efectuado em 2000 pela Faculdade de Direito da Columbia University concluiu que 68 por cento dos veredictos de pena de morte que ocorreram entre 1973 e 1995 continham falhas tão sérias que resultaram em novo julgamento ou nova sentença.

ब्लॉक 140
मकान 1243 से
WARNING
THIS BLDG HAS BEEN NOTIFIED AS DANGEROUS
ALL TRESSPASSERS ARE HEREBY WARNED
TO KEEP AWAY FROM THIS BLDG
AND RESPONSIPILITY FOR LOSS OF LIFE AND
PROPERTY LIES WITH THE DEFAULTERS
BY ORDER
EXECUTIVE ENGINEER MCD II / MUMBAI 37

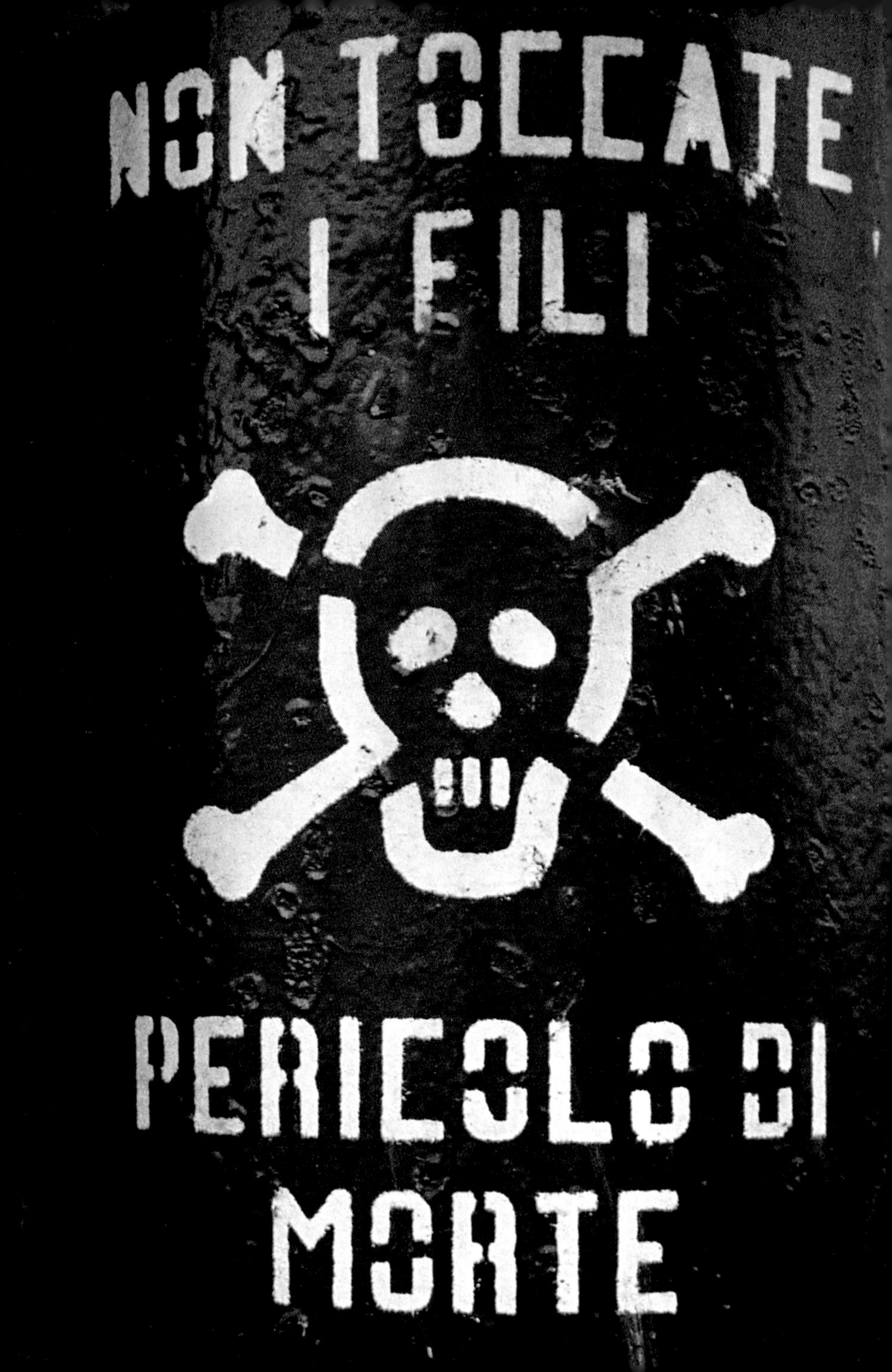
NON TOCCATE
I FILI
PERICOLO DI
MORTE

HUGO
ALTO
VOLTAJE
CARLOS

PERICOLO
DI MORTE

KABI
DANGER
HATARI
GANDA ELECTRICITY BOARD

DANGER
አደገኛ
S
T
R
246

NON TOCCATE I FILI
PERICOLO DI MORTE

CARICO

ALTA

YÜKSEK
VOLTAJ

380 V
СТОЙ!
ОПАСНО ДЛЯ
ЖИЗНИ

DANGER
HIGH VOLTAGE
KEEP OUT

GAS INFIAMMABILI

POZOR!
VISOKA NAPETOST
SMRTNO NEVARNO

CAUTION
FORK LIFT
TRUCKS IN
OPERATION

DANGE
Opening
in floor

Nevarnost
eksplozije !

Subterráneo
Sottoterra
Debaixo da terra

La ciudad australiana de Coober Pedy es conocida como la Capital Mundial del Ópalo. También es conocida por la poca afición de la población a registrarse en el censo, el bajo índice de votantes, la alta evasión fiscal, el juego y la bebida. Muchos de sus 4.000 residentes — que extraen el 70 por ciento de la producción mundial de ópalos— habitan en viviendas cavernícolas para huir del intenso calor que reina todo el año en esa zona. También existen albergues e iglesias subterráneos excavados por soldados de la Primera Guerra Mundial a su regreso de las trincheras. En las minas trabajan hombres de cuarenta y cinco nacionalidades distintas, aunque falta una: los aborígenes australianos, que en 1946 creyeron haber descubierto el mayor yacimiento de gemas pero han sido apartados del negocio y circulan a menudo por las calles mendigando. Los aborigenes han bautizado la ciudad *kupa piti*, o el *hoyo del hombre blanco*.

La cittadina australiana di Coober Pedy è nota come «la capitale mondiale dell'opale». Ma è anche famosa per la scarsa percentuale di risposte al censimento, la bassa affluenza alle urne, l'elevata evasione fiscale, la passione per il gioco d'azzardo e le sbronze. Molti dei suoi 4.000 abitanti – che estraggono il 70 per cento degli opali nel mondo – vivono in abitazioni ricavate dalle grotte per sfuggire all'intenso calore che si registra tutto l'anno nell'*outback* australiano. Sottoterra ci sono anche alberghi e chiese scavati dai soldati della Prima guerra mondiale al ritorno dalle trincee. Ben 45 nazionalità diverse lavorano fianco a fianco nelle miniere: mancano all'appello soltanto gli aborigeni... che scoprirono il più grande filone di gemme nel 1946. Esclusi dal lauto bottino, oggi sono ridotti a mendicare per strada. Loro hanno ribattezzato la città *kupa piti*, «il buco nella terra dell'uomo bianco».

A cidade australiana de Coober Pedy é conhecida como a «Capital das Opalas do Mundo.» Também é conhecida pelo seu baixo nível de recenseamento, por uma baixa participação eleitoral, uma fuga ao fisco elevada, o jogo e o alcoolismo. Muitos dos seus 4.000 residentes – que extraem 70 por cento das opalas do mundo – vivem em cavernas para escapar ao calor intenso do interior, que se sente durante todo o ano. Existem hotéis e igrejas subterrâneos, escavados por soldados da Primeira Guerra Mundial quando voltaram das trincheiras. Trabalham nas minas pessoas de quarenta e cinco nacionalidades, embora falte uma: os aborígines australianos, que embora tenham descoberto a maior mina de gemas em 1946, foram afastados da bonança, e encontram-se na sua maioria a pedir nas ruas. Chamam à cidade *kupa piti*, ou seja «buraco no solo pertencente ao homem branco.»

DANGER
DEEP
SHAFTS

PERICOLO DI CADUTA
APERTURA NEL SUOLO

AWAS LICIN

Halkrisk

BEWARE OF SHALLOW WATER WHEN DIVING

当心车辆

147

Aseos
Gabinetti
Casas da banho

Intocables
Intoccabili
Intocáveis

De los 1.000 millones de los habitantes de la India, 700 millones carecen de retretes decentes. Los hombres defecan donde y cuando les pilla; las mujeres se ven forzadas, por pudor, a adentrarse en los campos oscuros antes del amanecer y después del anochecer. En términos de higiene, la India es una fenomenal letrina al aire libre, con las consiguientes implicaciones sanitarias (cada ocho segundos muere un niño por une enfermedad relacionada con la falta de higiene pública). Para limpiarla están los basureros, integrantes de las castas indias más bajas (*bangii* o *dalit*), más conocidos como *intocables*. Descienden probablemente de antiguos prisioneros de guerra de las invasiones musulmanas. Alistados para limpiar las defecaciones de las mujeres veladas, que no podían abandonar su casa, los *intocables* vaciaban las *impurezas nocturnas* con las manos, y todavía sufren ese estigma. De ahí su categoría social de contaminados de los que siempre habrá gran demanda (la India tiene que tratar 135 millones de kilos de excrementos a diario). Más de 600.000 personas se siguen ganando la vida con la recogida de las impurezas nocturnas.

In India 700 milioni di persone, su una popolazione di un miliardo di abitanti, non possono usufruire di servizi sanitari decenti. Gli uomini si liberano l'intestino dove e quando capita; mentre le donne sono obbligate, per pudore, ad avventurarsi al buio nei campi prima dell'alba o dopo il tramonto. Il subcontinente indiano a livello igienico-sanitario è un'enorme latrina a cielo aperto, con le ovvie conseguenze per la salute (ogni otto secondi muore un bambino per malattie legate alle condizioni del sistema fognario). A ripulire ci pensano gli spazzini, che appartengono alle caste inferiori come i *bhangi* o i *dalit*. Meglio noti come gli «intoccabili», le loro origini risalgono a vari secoli fa, probabilmente ai prigionieri di guerra all'epoca delle invasioni musulmane. Incaricati di ripulire le feci delle donne *purdah*, che non potevano lasciare i propri alloggi, gli intoccabili svuotavano i pozzi neri a mani nude e ancora oggi devono liberarsi dallo stigma. Ciò spiega il loro status di contaminati e questo lavoro, per cui probabilmente la domanda non accennerà mai a diminuire, visto che in India si devono smaltire giornalmente ben 135 milioni di kg di escrementi. Più di 600.000 persone si guadagnano ancora da vivere rimuovendo le feci altrui.

Dos mil milhões de pessoas que vivem na Índia, 700 milhões não têm instalações sanitárias decentes. Os homens defecam em qualquer lugar e a qualquer altura; as mulheres são forçadas, por pudor, a fazê-lo em campos escuros antes do amanhecer e depois do pôr do sol. Em termos de higiene, a Índia é uma enorme latrina ao ar livre, com os seus consequentes efeitos para a saúde (morre uma criança a cada oito segundos de doenças relacionadas com a falta de saneamento). Estas limpezas são efectuadas por pessoas das castas mais baixas (Bhangi ou Dalit) da Índia, mais conhecidas por «intocáveis.» A sua origem provavelmente remonta aos prisioneiros de Guerra das invasões Muçulmanas, há séculos. Alistados para efectuar as limpezas das mulheres purdah que não podiam sair dos seus aposentos, os intocáveis esvaziavam os excrementos humanos com as próprias mãos, e ainda não recuperaram do estigma. Daí o seu estatuto de poluídos e um trabalho que pouco provavelmente deixará de ser necessário (a Índia tem 135 milhões de kg de excrementos para deitar fora todos os dias). Mais de 600.000 pessoas ainda ganham a vida a remover dejectos.

สุขาชาย

สุขาหญิง

च टाकूया.
पशु-पक्षां सारखी
घाण करु नका.
माणसा सारखे
जबाबदारीने वागा
आपला परिसर स्वच्छ
ठेवणे जरुरीचे आहे.

बृहन्मुंबई महानगरपालि
कचरा डब्यातच ट
अन्यथा दंड / कैद हो
तक्रार : ४१३५६८७

W

حمام الرجال
BAIN POUR HOMMES

WC

WC

حمام النساء
BAIN POUR FEMMES

161

¡No!

No!

Não!

Please switch

不准擺賣

ETATO FUMARE

NS OR ARCHERY

NO ENTRY

ห้ามหาบเร่

NO SCOOTERS

ห้ามวัตถุไวไฟ

MODEL AEROPLANES

BEER
WINE
WARNING

DON'T LITTER
PLEASE!
DEPARTMENT OF SANITATION
NOTICE
NO BALL PLAYING.
NO CARRIAGES.
NO PEDDLING.
NO LOITERING.
NO SITTING IN FRONT OF
BUILDING ALLOWED.

NO
DUMPING

O

O ENTR
嚴禁進入
RYODEN LIFT & ESCALATOR
菱電升降機有限
NOTICE
VIETATO
L`ACCESS
ห้ามเข้า
No Ent

火柴
禁带火种

et 92478 du 29 Mai

proibido
banho

Islet
CENTRAL BEACH
CAUTION
Swimmers/children are advised to swim within the Rope-in-area

ممنوع الانتظار
MOTOS
P DATES
1,3,5,7
COLORS
Yellow Pages
POLICIA
de 0 a 24 h
NO PARKIN
Horse-Drawn Carriages ONLY
ممنوع الانتظار

NEPAL ART GALLERY
MEHBOOB ARTS
बा.१ज
P

זהירות
עובדים
בדרך

179

Trabajo

Lavoro

Trabalho

Hombres trabajando
Lavori in corso
Homens a trabalhar

El futuro de la humanidad está bajo tierra. Los terrenos subterráneos son baratos, están protegidos de las intemperies, requieren poco consumo energético y están aislados de los rayos nocivos del sol. Estocolmo, que ya dispone de una sala de conciertos bajo tierra, prevé dotarse de calles subterráneas para peatones de aquí a fin de siglo. En la superpoblada Tokio, la gigantesca constructora japonesa Tokyu ha desvelado sus proyectos para Geotrópolis, una ciudad subterránea que será habitable en el año 2020. Otros lugares del mundo, como Escocia e Irlanda del Norte, están estudiando la posibilidad de conectarse mediante túneles submarinos.

La construcción subterránea creará muchos empleos para quienes tengan los conocimientos necesarios. Para aprender a manejar la maquinaria más avanzada para la construcción de túneles (gigantescos aparatos que excavan hasta 3,3 cm por minuto), busca empleo en uno de los subterráneos actualmente en construcción en distintas ciudades del mundo (Londres, París, El Cairo, Lisboa, Toronto, Brasilia y Roma; todas ellas tienen proyectos en curso). Como nos dijo Rafik Karaouzen, tunelero del metro de El Cairo, un aspirante a tunelero «no debe temer trabajar en espacios exiguos, calurosos y mal ventilados, ni debe importarle ensuciarse». Los sueldos son buenos comparados con casi todos los demás del ramo de la construcción, pero ¡ojo con los riesgos! La alta presión atmosférica en los túneles (a causa del aire que se les inyecta para impedir las filtraciones) puede causar enfermedades óseas y complicaciones pulmonares. El monóxido de carbono alcanza frecuentemente niveles peligrosos y la perforación de túneles suele cobrarse un muerto por cada 1,6 km.

Il futuro dell'umanità è sottoterra: i beni immobili sotterranei costano poco, sono al riparo dagli agenti atmosferici, fanno risparmiare energia e garantiscono un isolamento naturale contro i raggi nocivi del sole. Stoccolma, che ha già una sala per concerti sotterranea, prevede la creazione di corsie pedonali sottoterra entro la fine del secolo. A Tokyo, sovrappopolata fino a scoppiare, la colossale società di costruzioni Tokyu ha presentato dei progetti per una città sotterranea, Geotropolis, che sarà abitabile entro il 2020. E numerosi paesi, fra cui la Scozia e l'Irlanda del Nord, stanno progettando di collegarsi fra loro con dei tunnel sottomarini.

L'edilizia sotterranea creerà molti nuovi posti di lavoro per chi ha le giuste qualifiche. Per imparare a manovrare i più moderni macchinari per la costruzione di gallerie (scavatrici giganti che possono perforare fino a 3,3 cm di tunnel al minuto) cerca lavoro in una delle tante metropolitane in costruzione in tutto il mondo: Londra, Parigi, Il Cairo, Lisbona, Toronto, Brasilia e Roma hanno tutte dei progetti in corso. Come ci ha raccontato Rafik Karaouzen, che lavora nella metropolitana del Cairo, un aspirante scavagallerie «non deve aver paura di lavorare in luoghi chiusi, caldi e in spazi angusti, né preoccuparsi di sporcarsi.» La paga è allettante rispetto alla maggior parte dei lavori nel settore edile, ma attenzione ai rischi: l'elevata pressione atmosferica nei tunnel (dovuta all'aria pompata per evitare le infiltrazioni) può provocare malattie ossee e disturbi polmonari; il monossido di carbonio spesso raggiunge livelli pericolosi e in genere la costruzione di un tunnel semina dietro di sé un morto ogni 1,6 km.

O futuro da humanidade é debaixo da terra. O imobiliário subterrâneo é barato, resiste às in-

EN
CONSTRUCTION

tempéries, tem baixo consumo energético, e está protegido dos raios de sol perigosos. Estocolmo, que já possui uma sala de espectáculos subterrânea, está a planear passagens subterrâneas para peões antes do final do século. Com Tóquio a abrir pelas costuras, a companhia de construção gigante japonesa, Tokyu, desvendou desenhos para uma cidade subterrânea, a Geotropolis, pronta a habitar para o ano 2020. E dezenas de países, incluindo a Escócia e a Irlanda do Norte, estão a fazer planos para se ligarem através de túneis debaixo de água.

A construção subterrânea significará muitos empregos novos para as pessoas com as habilitações certas. Para aprender a utilizar o equipamento de escavações subterrâneas mais avançado (máquinas de escavação gigantes com diâmetro de escavação de até 3,3 cm de túnel por minuto), procura emprego num dos muitos metros agora em construção a nível mundial (Londres, Paris, Cairo, Lisboa, Toronto, Brasília e Roma têm todos projectos em curso). Como nos disse Rafik Karaouzen, um cavador de túneis do metro do Cairo, um potencial cavador de túneis «não deve ter medo de trabalhar em locais apertados, quentes e fechados, nem se importar de ficar sujo.» Os salários são bons em comparação com a maioria dos trabalhos da construção, mas deves estar ciente dos riscos: a elevada pressão atmosférica nos túneis (resultante do ar introduzido para evitar fugas) pode causar doenças dos ossos e problemas nos pulmões; o monóxido de carbono atinge frequentemente níveis perigosos; e a construção de túneis normalmente causa uma morte em cada 1,6 km.

KARAOKE
電気工事中
POWER UNDERCONSTRUCTION
TEPCO
ーブル 工事
ケーブル
工事中
ここより 100 m
11月30日まで
東京電力株式会
(株)関電工 銀座工務所
TEL03-5683-5
STRUCTION
菊池 誠司
~平成13年11月30日

VIETATO
L'ACCESSO
AI NON ADDETTI
VSTOP NEZAPOSLENIM
PREPOVEDAN
Förbjudet fö
obehöriga at
beträda

SOLO PERSONAL
AUTORIZADO

ALLUR AKSTUR
BANNAÐUR
- NEMA LÖGREGLA OG SLÖKKVILIÐ

END

Página/País/Fotógrafo
Pagina/Nazione/Fotografo
Página/País/Fotógrafo

Cover Hong Kong, Mandy Lee Jandrell
1 Australia, Paul Souders
6 Australia, Anne Cline
9 New Zealand, Jonathan Kress
11 Australia, Paul Souders
12 Sweden, Erik Undéhn
13 [1] Lithuania, Rasa Erentaite
13 [2] Slovenia, Borut Peterlin
13 [3] Denmark, Charlotte Østervang
13 [4] Bosnia-Herzegovina, Martin Kennedy
14 [1] Singapore, Jerry Lin
14 [2] India, Jodi Morrison
14 [3] Australia, Jorge Heijo
14 [4] Australia, Barbara Gurney
14 [5] USA, John Cunningham
14 [6] South Africa, Garth Walker
15 Hong Kong, Mandy Lee Jandrell
16 Santa Lucia, L. Glennie
17 Australia, Jorge Heijo
18 Colombia, James Mollison
19 Chile, Paul Souders
20 Canada, Valerie Williams
22 USA, Patrice Hanicotte
25 Indonesia, Rahmat Buwantoro
27 Denmark, Anders Ulrik
28 [1] Czech Republic, Julie Denesha
28 [2] Italy, Marco Callegari
28 [3] Indonesia, Rahmat Buwantoro
28 [4] Laos, Tom Ridgway
29 [1] Lithuania, Rasa Erentaite
29 [2] Israel, Dana Levy
29 [3] The Netherlands, Tyler Whisnand
29 [4] Singapore, Jerry Lin
30 [1] Thailand, Nick Nostitz
30 [2] USA, Stefan Ruiz
30 [3] Ireland, Eoin O'Mahony
30 [4] Malaysia, Roland Takeshi
31 Honduras, Kim Naylor
32 Serbia-Montenegro, Dejan Djuric and Djordje Nenadovic
33 Canada, Valerie Williams
34 Canada, Krystel Wallet
35 USA, Robert Young Pelton
38 Namibia, Bernd Meyer
40 [1] Colombia, Alejandro Duque
40 [2] USA, Adrianna Linderman
40 [3] Pakistan, Amean Mohammed
40 [4] Thailand, Nick Nostitz
40 [5] Irak, Rose George
40 [6] South Korea, Arthur Binard
40 [7] Hong Kong, Mandy Lee Jandrell
40 [8] Turkey, Gurdal Tezvar
40 [9] Canada, Valerie Williams
41 [1] Ethiopia, Tefera Ghedamu
41 [2] Morocco, Mattias Zoppellaro
41 [3] Spain, Carlos Mustienes
41 [4] Thailand, Guy Saville
41 [5] Laos, S. Galt
41 [6] Laos, S. Galt
41 [7] Cambodia, Tom Ridgway
41 [8] Kenya, James Mollison
41 [9] Italy, Marco Callegari
42 The Netherlands, Suse Uhman
45 Belgium, Ben Latto
46 [1] India, Rajesh Vora
46 [2] Australia, Jasmin Chua
47 [1] South Africa, Garth Walker
47 [2] Italy, Carlos Mustienes
48 South Africa, Darnell Sardinha
49 France, James Mollison
50 [1] Canada, Valerie Williams
50 [2] Brazil, Juliana Stein
50 [3] Turkey, Gurdal Tezvar
50 [4] Ireland, Eoin O'Mahony
51 [1] Australia, Barbara Gurney
51 [2] Lithuania, Rasa Erentaite
51 [3] Italy, Suse Uhman
51 [4] Italy, Michela Beccacece
52 [1] France, James Mollison
52 [2] France, James Mollison
52 [3] France, Martino Sorteni
53 [1] UK, Guy Wheeler
53 [2] Italy, Suse Uhman
53 [3] Austria, Stefan Russel
53 [4] France, James Mollison
54 Denmark, Charlotte Østervang
57 [1] New Zealand, Jonathan Kress
57 [2] Ecuador, Kai Zimmermann
57 [3] Brazil, Juliana Stein
57 [4] USA, Stefan Ruiz
58 Brazil, Juliana Stein
59 USA, Chris Lane
60 Argentina, Esteban Pastorino
61 [1] New Zealand, Jonathan Kress
61 [2] New Zealand, Jonathan Kress
62 Italy, Marco Callegari
63 Russia, Lucy Grin
64 South Africa, Sadhna Baskali
66 Brazil, Juliana Stein
69 Russia, Lucy Grin
70 [1] Lithuania, Rasa Erentaite
70 [2] Mexico, Neli Ruzic
70 [3] Japan, Arthur Binard
70 [4] Ethiopia, Tefera Ghedamu
70 [5] Taiwan, Duncan Moore and Marion Smallbones
70 [6] The Netherlands, Tyler Whisnand
70 [7] The Netherlands, Tyler Whisnand
70 [8] Ireland, Eoin O'Mahony
70 [9] Laos, S. Galt
70 [10] Brazil, Juliana Stein
70 [11] Russia, Lucy Grin
70 [12] Brazil, Juliana Stein
71 Brazil, John Maier
72 [1] Indonesia, Rahmat Buwantoro
72 [2] France, Patrice Hannicotte
72 [3] Russia, James Mollison
72 [4] Cyprus, Gunnar Svanberg
72 [5] Colombia, Alejandro Duque
72 [6] Ecuador, Kai Zimmermann
72 [7] Slovenia, Borut Peterlin
72 [8] Thailand, Guy Saville
72 [9] Russia, Lucy Grin
73 Pakistan, James Mollison
74 Guinea, James Mollison
75 Ecuador, Kai Zimmermann
77 Bulgaria, Boris Missirkov and Georgi Bogdanov
78 Laos, Tom Ridgway
79 [1] Italy, Paulo Condez
79 [2] Japan, Arthur Binard
79 [3] Hong Kong, Mandy Lee Jandrell
79 [4] Laos, S. Galt
80 China, James Mollison
81 [1] Ethiopia, Tefera Ghedamu
81 [2] Cambodia, Tim and Sophie Loft
82 Indonesia, Rahmat Buwantoro
84 The Netherlands, Tyler Whisnand
85 [1] Switzerland, Martino Sorteni
85 [2] Denmark, Charlotte Østervang
86 Japan, James Mollison
87 [1] Russia, Lucy Grin
87 [2] Ireland, Eoin O'Mahony
87 [3] The Netherlands, Tyler Whisnand
87 [4] Canada, Valerie Williams
87 [5] The Netherlands, Tyler Whisnand
87 [6] France, Grégoire Basdevant
87 [7] The Netherlands, Tyler Whisnand
87 [8] Singapore, Jerry Lin
87 [9] Ireland, Eoin O'Mahony
87 [10] Italy, Marco Callegari
87 [11] Denmark, Charlotte Østervang
87 [12] Germany, Parag Kapashi
88 India, Rajesh Vora
90 Argentina, Esteban Pastorino
92 [1] Uruguay, Lucía Bruno
92 [2] Mexico, Ben Latto
92 [3] Honduras, Kim Naylor
92 [4] New Zealand, Jonathan Kress

93 [1] Ireland, Eoin O'Mahony
93 [2] Ecuador, Kai Zimmermann
93 [3] Canada, Krystel Wallet
93 [4] Brazil, Juliana Stein
94 Italy, Marco Callegari
95 [1] Puerto Rico, Alvaro Silva
95 [2] Mexico, Neli Ruzic
96 New Zealand, Jonathan Kress
97 Japan, James Mollison
99 Cambodia, James Mollison
100 Sierra Leone, James Mollison
101 Ivory Coast, James Mollison
102 [1] Democratic Republic of Kongo, James Mollison
102 [2] Czech Republic, Julie Denesha
102 [3] Cameroon, James Mollison
102 [4] Kenya, James Mollison
103 [1] Pakistan, Amean Mohammed
103 [2] China, James Mollison
103 [3] Italy, Marco Callegari
103 [4] The Netherlands, Tyler Whisnand
106 Slovenia, Borut Peterlin
107 Bulgaria, O. Pearson
108 Egypt, Grégoire Basdevant
109 India, Rajesh Vora
110 USA, Stefan Ruiz
112 India, Simon Saliot
113 USA, Esteban Pastorino
114 [1] New Zealand, Jonathan Kress
114 [2] Ireland, Eoin O'Mahony
114 [3] Malaysia, Roland Takeshi
114 [4] Ireland, Eoin O'Mahony
114 [5] Canada, Valerie Williams
114 [6] Canada, Valerie Williams
114 [7] Egypt, Claudia Wiens
114 [8] Thailand, Nick Nostitz
114 [9] New Zealand, Jonathan Kress
114 [10] New Zealand, Jonathan Kress
114 [11] New Zealand, Jonathan Kress
114 [12] Honduras, Naylor Kim
115 USA, Stefan Ruiz
116 Australia, Jorge Heijo
117 [1] Honduras, Kim Naylor
117 [2] Honduras, Kim Naylor
117 [3] Honduras, Kim Naylor
117 [4] Ireland, Eoin O'Mahony
117 [5] Thailand, Nick Nostitz
117 [6] Mexico, Neli Ruzic
117 [7] New Zealand, Jonathan Kress
118 Thailand, Nick Nostitz
120 [1] New Zealand, Jonathan Kress
120 [2] Taiwan, Duncan Moore and Marion Smallbones
120 [3] Pakistan, Amean Mohammed
120 [4] Egypt, Grégoire Basdevant
120 [5] Serbia-Montenegro, Dejan Djuric and Djorgje Nenadovic
120 [6] Taiwan, Duncan Moore and Marion Smallbones
120 [7] USA, Robert Young Pelton
120 [8] Mexico, Neli Ruzic
120 [9] Serbia-Montenegro, Dejan Djuric and Djorgje Nenadovic
120 [10] India, Neha Diddee
120 [11] Spain, Carlos Mustienes
120 [12] New Zealand, Jonathan Kress
121 Colombia, Alejandro Duque
122 Mexico, Neli Ruzic
125 Democratic Republic of Congo, James Mollison
127 India, Rajesh Vora
128 Italy, James Mollison
129 [1] Mexico, Grégoire Basdevant
129 [2] Italy, Boris Missirkov and Georgi Bogdanov
130 [1] Uganda, Julius Ananura
130 [2] Ethiopia, Tefera Ghedamu
130 [3] Italy, Marco Callegari
131 Russia, James Mollison
132 Canada, Valerie Williams
133 Canada, Valerie Williams
134 [1] Italy, Marco Callegari
134 [2] Slovenia, Borut Peterlin
134 [3] Ireland, Eoin O'Mahony
134 [4] Ireland, Eoin O'Mahony
135 Slovenia, Borut Peterlin
137 Australia, Paul Souders
138 [1] Italy, Martino Sorteni
138 [2] Indonesia, Rahmat Buwantoro
139 Sweden, Erik Undéhn
140 USA, Jacob Langvad
141 Australia, Stefan Ruiz
142 China, Christine Pemberton
143 Italy, Marco Callegari
144 Slovenia, Borut Peterlin
146 Mexico, Neli Ruzic
149 India, Rajesh Vora
150 Thailand, Carlos Mustienes
152 India, Rajesh Vora
154 Italy, James Mollison
156 Morocco, Suse Uhman
158 [1] Morocco, Grégoire Basdevant
158 [2] Croatia, Boris Missirkov and Georgi Bognadov
158 [3] France, Grégoire Basdevant
158 [4] Italy, Carlos Mustienes
158 [5] Lithuania, Rasa Erentaite
158 [6] Russia, Lucy Grin
158 [7] Lebanon, Nadim Asfar
159 [1] France, James Mollison
159 [2] Lithuania, Rasa Erentaite
159 [3] Austria, Marco Callegari
159 [4] Lithuania, Rasa Erentaite
159 [5] Morocco, Grégoire Basdevant
159 [6] Laos, S. Galt
160 Hong Kong, Mandy Lee Jandrell
162 [1] UK, Stefan Ruiz
162 [2] Australia, Jorge Heijo
162 [3] Canada, Krystel Wallet
162 [4] Puerto Rico, Alvaro Silva
162 [5] Italy, Boris Missirkov and Georgi Bogdanov
162 [6] Germany, Francesca Jacchia
162 [7] USA, Adrianna Linderman
162 [8] Germany, Francesca Jacchia
162 [9] Italy, Suse Uhman
163 [10] South Africa, Garth Walker
163 [11] Russia, Lucy Grin
163 [12] Australia, Jorge Heijo
164 [1] Hong Kong, James Mollison
164 [2] Brazil, Juliana Stein
164 [3] Italy, Marco Callegari
164 [4] Australia, Jorge Heijo
164 [5] Hong Kong, Lan Ko Sui
164 [6] Belgium, Ben Latto
164 [7] Italy, Marco Callegari
164 [8] Italy, Carlos Mustienes
164 [9] Hungary, András Hajdu
164 [10] Australia, Jorge Heijo
164 [11] Australia, Jorge Heijo
164 [12] Hungary, András Hajdu
165 [1] France, Stefan Ruiz
165 [2] USA, Robert Young Pelton
165 [3] France, Grégoire Basdevant
165 [4] Japan, James Mollison
165 [5] Bosnia-Herzegovina, Carlos Mustienes
165 [6] South Africa, Garth Walker
165 [7] Thailand, Tim and Sophie Loft
165 [8] Hungary, András Hajdu
165 [9] USA, Carlos Mustienes
165 [10] Australia, Jorge Heijo
165 [11] Australia, Jorge Heijo
165 [12] Thailand, Carlos Mustienes
166 USA, Grégoire Basdevant
168 Kenya, James Mollison
170 [1] Ireland, Eoin O'Mahony
170 [2] China, Patrizia Benvenuti
170 [3] Italy, Boris Missirkov and Georgi Bogdanov

170 [4] Hungary, András Hajdu
170 [5] Cyprus, Gunnar Svanberg
170 [6] Italy, Marco Callegari
170 [7] Denmark, Charlotte Østervang
170 [8] Russia, Lucy Grin
170 [9] Thailand, Tim and Sophie Loft
171 Belgium, James Mollison
172 Hong Kong, Mandy Lee Jandrell
173 [1] Russia, James Mollison
173 [2] Italy, Marco Callegari
173 [3] China, Patrizia Benvenuti
173 [4] France, Stefan Ruiz
173 [5] South Africa, Garth Walker
173 [6] Iceland, Gunnar Svanberg
173 [7] Singapore, Jerry lin
173 [8] Russia, Lucy Grin
173 [9] Irak, Rose George
173 [10] Iceland, Gunnar Svanberg
173 [11] Egypt, Grégoire Basdevant
173 [12] UK, Guy Wheeler
174 Brazil, Juliana Stein
175 Singapore, Jerry Lin
176 [1] Egypt, Grégoire Basdevant
176 [2] Canada, Valerie Williams
176 [3] Puerto Rico, Alvaro Silva
176 [4] India, Diddee Neha
176 [5] Spain, Grégoire Basdevant
176 [6] Uganda, Julius Ananura
176 [7] Ireland, Eoin O'Mahony
176 [8] Pakistan, Amean Mohammed
176 [9] Egypt, Claudia Wiens
177 India, Alex Lebeaun
178 Israel, Dana Levy
181 Canada, Krystel Wallet
183 Japan, James Mollison
184 [1] Italy, Marco Callegari
184 [2] Slovenia, Borut Peterlin
184 [3] Turkey, Gurdal Tezvar
184 [4] Sweden, Erik Undéhn
185 Ecuador, Kim Naylor
186 [1] Laos, Grégoire Basdevant
186 [2] Iceland, Gunnar Svanberg
187 Ireland, Eoin O'Mahony

Back Cover

[1] Lithuania, Rasa Erentaite
[2] Mexico, Neli Ruzic
[3] Japan, Arthur Binard
[4] Ethiopia, Tefera Ghedamu
[5] Taiwan, Duncan Moore and Marion Smallbones
[6] The Netherlands, Tyler Whisnand
[7] The Netherlands, Tyler Whisnand
[8] Ireland, Eoin O'Mahony
[9] Laos, S. Galt
[10] Brazil, Juliana Stein
[11] Russia, Lucy Grin
[12] Brazil, Juliana Stein

Endpapers

Front South Africa, Sadhna Baskali
Back Australia, Jorge Heijo
[1] Honduras, Kim Naylor
[2] Honduras, Kim Naylor
[3] Honduras, Kim Naylor
[4] Ireland, Eoin O'Mahony
[5] Thailand, Nick Nostitz
[6] Mexico, Neli Ruzic
[7] New Zealand, Jonathan Kress

SIGNS is a project by COLORS Magazine

To stay informed about upcoming TASCHEN titles,
please request our magazine at www.taschen.com/magazine or write to TASCHEN, Hohenzollernring 53, D-50672 Cologne, Germany, contact@taschen.com, Fax: +49-221-254919. We will be happy to send you a free copy of our magazine which is filled with information about all of our books.

Editors Carlos Mustienes and Thomas Hilland
Art Director Marco Callegari
Co editor Giuliana Rando
Associate editors Samantha Bartoletti and Grégoire Basdevant
Editorial coordination Thierry Nebois
Text editor Tom Ridgway
Spanish editors Clara Cabarrocas and Fernando Linares
Italian editor Giovanna Gatteschi
Portuguese editor Monica Roncon

Editorial director Renzo di Renzo

Production Marco Callegari
Lithography Sartori Group S.r.l.
Thank you Bruno Ceschel, Giovanna Dunmall, Sara Gaiotto, Rose George, Michele Lunardi, Michael Medelin, Loris Pasetto, Renzo Saccaro, Claudio Sartori, Janine Stephen, Suzanne Wales, Fiona Wilson.

Printed in Italy
ISBN 978–3-8228-4840-1

Graphic Design for the 21st Century
Eds. Charlotte & Peter Fiell /
Flexi-cover, 192 pp. / € 6.99 /
$ 9.99 / £ 5.99 / ¥ 1.500

Design of the 20th Century
Eds. Charlotte & Peter Fiell /
Flexi-cover, 192 pp. / € 6.99 /
$ 9.99 / £ 5.99 / ¥ 1.500

Design for the 21st Century
Eds. Charlotte & Peter Fiell /
Flexi-cover, 192 pp. / € 6.99 /
$ 9.99 / £ 5.99 / ¥ 1.500

"These books are beautiful objects, well-designed and lucid." —*Le Monde*, Paris, on the ICONS series

---

"Buy them all and add some pleasure to your life."

60s Fashion
Ed. Jim Heimann
70s Fashion
Ed. Jim Heimann
African Style
Ed. Angelika Taschen
Alchemy & Mysticism
Alexander Roob
American Indian
Dr. Sonja Schierle
Angels
Gilles Néret
Architecture Now!
Ed. Philip Jodidio
Art Now
Eds. Burkhard Riemschneider, Uta Grosenick
Atget's Paris
Ed. Hans Christian Adam
Bamboo Style
Ed. Angelika Taschen
Ingrid Bergman
Ed. Paul Duncan, Scott Eyman
Berlin Style
Ed. Angelika Taschen
Humphrey Bogart
Ed. Paul Duncan, James Ursini
Marlon Brando
Ed. Paul Duncan, F.X. Feeney
Brussels Style
Ed. Angelika Taschen
Cars of the 50s
Ed. Jim Heimann, Tony Thacker
Cars of the 60s
Ed. Jim Heimann, Tony Thacker
Cars of the 70s
Ed. Jim Heimann, Tony Thacker
Charlie Chaplin
Ed. Paul Duncan, David Robinson
China Style
Ed. Angelika Taschen
Christmas
Ed. Jim Heimann, Steven Heller
Design Handbook
Charlotte & Peter Fiell
Design for the 21st Century
Eds. Charlotte & Peter Fiell
Design of the 20th Century
Eds. Charlotte & Peter Fiell
Marlene Dietrich
Ed. Paul Duncan, James Ursini
Devils
Gilles Néret
Robert Doisneau
Ed. Jean-Claude Gautrand
East German Design
Ralf Ulrich/Photos: Ernst Hedler
Clint Eastwood
Ed. Paul Duncan, Douglas Keesey
Egypt Style
Ed. Angelika Taschen
Encyclopaedia Anatomica
Ed. Museo La Specola Florence
M.C. Escher
Fashion
Ed. The Kyoto Costume Institute
Fashion Now!
Eds. Terry Jones, Susie Rushton
Fruit
Ed. George Brookshaw, Uta Pellgrü-Gagel
HR Giger
HR Giger
Grand Tour
Harry Seidler
Cary Grant
Ed. Paul Duncan, F.X. Feeney
Graphic Design
Eds. Charlotte & Peter Fiell
Greece Style
Ed. Angelika Taschen
Halloween
Ed. Jim Heimann, Steven Heller
Havana Style
Ed. Angelika Taschen
Audrey Hepburn
Ed. Paul Duncan, F.X. Feeney
Katharine Hepburn
Ed. Paul Duncan, Alain Silver
Homo Art
Gilles Néret
Hot Rods
Ed. Coco Shinomiya, Tony Thacker
Hula
Ed. Jim Heimann
India Bazaar
Samantha Harrison, Bari Kumar
London Style
Ed. Angelika Taschen
Steve McQueen
Ed. Paul Duncan, Alain Silver
Mexico Style
Ed. Angelika Taschen
Miami Style
Ed. Angelika Taschen
Minimal Style
Ed. Angelika Taschen
Marilyn Monroe
Ed. Paul Duncan, F.X. Feeney
Morocco Style
Ed. Angelika Taschen
New York Style
Ed. Angelika Taschen
Paris Style
Ed. Angelika Taschen
Penguin
Frans Lanting
20th Century Photography
Museum Ludwig Cologne
Pierre et Gilles
Eric Troncy
Provence Style
Ed. Angelika Taschen
Robots & Spaceships
Ed. Teruhisa Kitahara
Safari Style
Ed. Angelika Taschen
Seaside Style
Ed. Angelika Taschen
Signs
Ed. Julius Wiedeman
South African Style
Ed. Angelika Taschen
Starck
Philippe Starck
Surfing
Ed. Jim Heimann
Sweden Style
Ed. Angelika Taschen
Tattoos
Ed. Henk Schiffmacher
Tiffany
Jacob Baal-Teshuva
Tokyo Style
Ed. Angelika Taschen
Tuscany Style
Ed. Angelika Taschen
Valentines
Ed. Jim Heimann, Steven Heller
Web Design: Best Studios
Ed. Julius Wiedemann
Web Design: Best Studios 2
Ed. Julius Wiedemann
Web Design: E-Commerce
Ed. Julius Wiedemann
Web Design: Flash Sites
Ed. Julius Wiedemann
Web Design: Music Sites
Ed. Julius Wiedemann
Web Design: Portfolios
Ed. Julius Wiedemann
Orson Welles
Ed. Paul Duncan, F.X. Feeney
Women Artists in the 20th and 21st Century
Ed. Uta Grosenick

ICONS